Neeka the Kestrel

By the same author

THE WHITE COLT

Neeka the Kestrel

written and illustrated by
DAVID ROOK

Walker and Company
New York

© DAVID ROOK 1967

First published in the United States
of America in 1968 by Walker and
Company, a division of the Walker
Publishing Company, Inc.

Library of Congress Catalog Card
Number: 68—26543.

Printed in Great Britain
by UNWIN BROTHERS of Woking

Chapter One

IN Alora, during the long summer evenings, the swifts wheel over the rooftops. Above them, so high that the low sun gilds their wings, the lesser kestrels circle and soar. Throughout the day these little falcons come and go from their nests, bringing food for their young; but in the evening they fly high, filling the sky with dozens of floating silver crosses. Impossible to think of Alora without seeing and hearing in my imagination their beautiful flight and their wild hawk-voices, ringing out over the screaming of the swifts. Hardly surprising, when I decided at last to keep a falcon, that I should go to Alora to find it.

Alora (stress on the first syllable: *AL*ora) is a bustling country village, about twenty miles inland from Malaga. Like most of the villages in Andalucia it is white with terra cotta roofs and narrow cobbled streets. Like many others it is dominated by a derelict Moorish fort, built in the 12th century. The old fort stands at the top of a steep hill and the village spreads beneath it like a white shawl. The Guadalhorce flows past the foot of the hill with its broad ribbon of orange and lemon groves, a fertile green causeway leading south towards the sea. Overshadowing the hill, around which the village clings, is a great pile of rock called 'el hacho', the Sphinx, for its brooding shape. From here towards the north-west the sierras rise and fall like waves, with Ronda balanced precariously on the crest of the highest wave. The landscape is full of colour, but green plays a minor role: apart from the river valley there are only the dry dusty greens of the olive and the almond trees, the grey-green of the prickly pear and the pita. All else is rock and the dusty soil.

When I arrived in Alora last May it was with the intention of 'taking' a lesser kestrel. It was not difficult to find a nest: there were at least five in the bell-tower of the church, only yards from my bedroom window. I was able to watch the feeding of one of the broods going on all day, with a siesta of course; even the birds observe the siesta. But I went further afield, to the fort at the top of the hill, now a cemetery. There were numerous nests in holes in the crumbling walls, but one in particular proved easily accessible: the nest at the top of the old watch-tower, the highest point in the

whole village. A stairway took me most of the way, a little scrambling the rest of the way, and I was at the top of the tower with the whole of the surrounding countryside spread out before me.

But I had no eyes for the view this time for there, in front of me, was the nest. Two of the young kestrels were huddled together on the ledge, while the third was on its own to one side. All three watched me approach, wide-eyed and unblinking. As I arrived at the nest they took up defensive positions: sitting back on their tails, one foot raised threateningly. At the same time they hissed like snakes, and their eyes never wavered.

They were, as far as I could judge, just about fully-fledged. That is, they had their full complement of adult feathers. Only wisps of creamy down on their heads and backs showed how recently-acquired was their plumage. Clearly the moment to take my bird was there and then, for they would soon have left the nest altogether. As to which of the three I would take there was never any doubt: the independent one on the ledge was almost perfect, hardly a trace of down remained, and she was a little bigger than the other two. As I stretched out my hand she scolded me sharply and raised both her feet, but with my hand only inches away she changed her tactics: in a flurry of dust she righted herself and launched out into space.

Apart from flapping around the nest-area she could hardly have flown before, for it would have been impossible to return. In spite of this, she made a gallant try: wings beating purposefully she flew outwards, though quite rapidly downwards, away from the walls of the fort.

It was fortunate that I had an assistant at the foot of the tower; Paquito was fifteen years old and nimble, and immediately gave chase. Had the tower been on level ground the eyas would not have got very far, but as it happened her angle of descent was almost the same as the gradient of the hill as it fell away from the fort at the top.

Given limitless stamina she might even have reached the river, almost a mile away, but about half-way down the hill she appeared to tire. A faltering in her steady flapping presaged a sudden and undignified belly-flop into a clump of broom, and there Paquito caught her.

When he arrived, breathless, at the top of the hill, she was firmly held in his right hand, panting still from the effort of her flight. Paquito showed me his free hand, grinning ruefully: it was bleeding where she had bitten him. The rich chestnut of her back-feathers was filmed with a layer of white dust, but her eyes were a clear ebony.

All the way back to the house, down through the narrow streets, people craned to see what Paquito held so carefully before him, while a growing retinue of children ran and screamed behind. I watched her anxiously: her beak closed now, she appeared

3

almost comfortable in the enclosing hand. Her brilliant eyes continued to survey calmly. If she blinked, even once, I did not see it.

The *Manual of Falconry* decreed a room or a shed for the first stage of her training, but this was not possible. When we arrived at the house it was already late afternoon and Paquito had to go to work in the evening. We made her as comfortable as possible in a beer-crate covered by another beer-crate. At least it was well ventilated.

During the evening I could not resist going to look at her three or four times. In the half-light it was difficult to see her; only her eyes showed, gazing up at me steadily from the shadow in the corner of the crate. And it was during this evening that I chose a name for her. The Spanish word for 'kestrel' is a pretty one: 'Cerníçalo'. The stress falls on the second syllable, making it 'thair-*NEE*-kalo'. Out of that came simply *NEE*-ka. *Neeka*.

There followed an interlude of ten days before I was due to return to England. Because of the lack of room, I was unable to start Neeka's training there and then, so was lent a large bird-cage, about three feet square by two feet deep, and this had to serve. She was placed into it in a flurry of wings and screaming and left to get used to it before being fed.

After two days of roaming about the establishment, the cage finally came to rest in an ideal place: amongst the branches of an apple tree in the orchard. Here she was able to see, through the leaves, a certain amount of coming and going which would begin to accustom her to the proximity of people. It was in the shade all day, which was vital, for falcons do not like too much direct sunlight. She was fed morning and evening on scraps of meat, chicken-necks and so on, and soon came to know her meal-times. This idyll was interrupted only once when I found her one day hopping from foot to foot and gazing anxiously at a stream of large ants which were engaged in carrying off the remains of her last meal. After this we hung the cage from an overhead branch and the problem did not recur. By the time I was ready to leave Spain she was showing faint signs of recognition and/or enthusiasm when I showed up with her meat. The journey to England destroyed that little evidence of progress.

She had to travel in a cardboard box, there was no other way. Properly, I should have made her a strong crate and sent her by air-freight, but she was so small. In the end she went, still protesting violently, into a square cardboard box, lined with sacking and pierced with innumerable holes for ventilation. It was lunchtime when we left, and very hot.

She remained fairly quiet during the drive down to Malaga, but came to life on the four-hour coach journey to La Linea. At regular intervals she assaulted the walls of her prison, so that the box rocked on the seat beside me. At eleven o'clock that night, some

six or seven hours later, her attacks were weakening and the intervals of peace were lengthening. Soon after midnight the box was beneath my seat in the overnight Viscount, and she was silent from the moment the engines started up.

On arrival at Heathrow I was the last to leave the aircraft. The cabin crew were looking at the bulky cardboard box with unabashed curiosity, so I stopped to explain its contents. I even tried to explain how Neeka would be able to dine out on having flown fifteen hundred miles non-stop before really leaving the nest, but this was too much for them and I left in a blank silence.

There was some embarrassment on the coach too, from the airport to the terminal. Neeka awoke, apparently refreshed, and renewed the attack, achieving some success this time by breaching a hole in one corner. Every time there was a flurry of wings, accompanied by muffled curses, passengers turned round and stared as I huddled at the back. By the time I finally got her to her new home, at about 11.00 a.m., I hardly needed to open the box: Neeka was as good as out through the side.

Chapter Two

HER home for the first period of training was to be a shed in my parents' garden. I had been unable to find a place for much of its contents and there was a lot of cover for anything small which might have wanted to hide. She disappeared into it as though meaning never to reappear, scuttling across the floor into the nearest shadows.

That was my first mistake: I had not fitted her jesses. These are the pieces of soft leather, about six inches long, which were to be attached to her legs. That night, with the aid of a powerful torch, I tried to find her in order to fit them. After fifteen minutes or so I was in a panic, asking myself how she could possibly have escaped. In the end however, she was somewhere ridiculous: behind something or beneath something that could never have concealed a fully-grown bird. Although she hissed at the torch, she lay quietly in my bare hand, and did not resist when I put a sock over her head and shoulders to keep her quiet while putting on the jesses. With the aid of my father this took a couple of minutes and we returned her to the shed. Again she scuttled off into the darkness, this time with the jesses flapping behind her.

For some days I saw very little of her. If I crept up to the door and peeped in I might see her sunning herself on the floor or perching on an old trunk, but as soon as she saw me she would scuttle off to cover, looking more like a large mouse than a small falcon.

Each day, at morning and evening, I left a board with pieces of meat on it. After three or four days I discovered her favourite hiding place: at the corner of the old trunk on which she would often perch, in a little gap between a wooden box and the wall. When I first saw her there she was crammed back into the corner staring out at me suspiciously. When I went a little too close up came one foot and she hissed fiercely, but I was well satisfied for now at last I could begin to tame her.

This training process, in the case of hawks, is known as 'manning' and it is thus that I shall refer to it from now on. One evening, perhaps a week after her arrival, I took her food in to her and closed the door behind me. I settled down beside the trunk and

looked into her corner. Two hostile eyes stared back out of the shadow. I had prepared a thin piece of bamboo, a couple of feet long, and on the thin end of this I impaled a small piece of meat. As slowly as I could I moved the baited end of the cane towards her. In spite of my care she took up a defensive posture and started to hiss. With frequent pauses I inched the meat towards her, holding it at the level of her beak, wide open now as she faced the apparent threat. At last the meat arrived within inches of her face: with a movement so fast that I could hardly see it she shot out one foot, snatched at the meat and returned to her position, leaving the meat lying in front of her. I pulled the cane back slowly and repeated the operation, and continued to repeat the operation. A quarter of an hour later we had arrived at the point where I could get the meat right up to her. She was now twitching it off with her beak and then ignoring it. In front of her lay seven or eight pieces, untouched. At last the break-through came. After sitting for almost a minute glaring at the tit-bit in front of her, she took it neatly and swallowed it. She accepted the last two pieces in the same way and I left her to clear up what was in front of her.

This 'manning' business is basically a matter of going a fraction further each day, as is most animal training; introducing innovations gradually until they are accepted and absorbed. So it was with Neeka, twice a day every day, until finally she would take the meat from the stick every time, without hissing.

Her gradual relaxation towards me was beginning to show in other ways too: I could arrive and watch her over the door as she perched on her trunk. She would look back at me calmly and would only scuttle for cover when I began to enter the shed.

Now for another hurdle. One evening I left the cane where it was and settled down in my usual place. She was in her 'lair' but no longer crammed into the corner: she was standing looking out expectantly. I took a piece of meat, laid it over the forefinger of my right hand and started moving it towards her, almost imperceptibly. It seemed to take long minutes—it may have done for all I know. As my hand approached her I watched for danger signals: her feathers were down as tight as could be, but her beak was closed. As my hand covered the last few inches she sat back on her tail ready to defend herself, but still she did not hiss or strike out. At last my finger was there in front of her. She hesitated for a matter of seconds then took the meat and swallowed it. Jubilantly I gave her the rest of her meal in the same way. Two days later she was taking meat from my fingers out in the open, on the top of the trunk, and I could enter the shed and move around—so long as I was quiet—without disturbing her.

During this period she was, in the old language of falconry, a ramager (old French: 'rammage') which is to say she was free to fly up to branches or perching places within the confines of her shed. That she was making use of this privilege became obvious one morning: when I looked in she was not on her favourite trunk, and it was some time before I saw her. She was perching cheerfully on the top of a step-ladder, at least five feet from the floor. She could not have climbed there; she could only have flown there.

At this favourable point the poor bird was stuffed into a large cardboard box and transported to another home, for the second time in her short life. That this was unfortunate I knew, for she went back several days in her progress; but it was necessary, for I could no longer delay moving back to my cottage in Leicestershire.

In spite of the set-back it was still a good move, for here she had a whole upstairs room to herself, and open country all round. She soon grew accustomed to her new surroundings and selected the window-sill as her perch. From here she would gaze out of the window all day, watching everything in the landscape that moved. Contrary to usage, I did not dim her mews but let the daylight in.

As soon as she was settled in I made her a screen perch. This was a length of wood, about four inches square and three feet in length, set between two uprights at a height of about three feet, six inches. This brought it a few inches above the level of the

window-sill—an important point, as will be seen in a moment. I left this perch a couple of feet from the window so that she could become used to it; sure enough, on the second morning, she was perching on it in preference to the window-sill.

Now, a brief interlude of hawk-psychology. If a hawk is left in a room with a choice of perching-places, it will always select the highest, provided that it is comfortable. Similarly, if a hawk is out of doors on its weathering-block (described later), it will be uneasy if it is placed close to a fence or a post higher than the block, and will probably make repeated attempts to fly up to it. Using this fact, I got Neeka onto her perch, where I wanted her, by making it a little higher than her window-sill and placing it nearby, thus making it preferable to her previous place.

By this time she had come a long way towards accepting me; I could move around the room and feed her from the hand without frightening her. I decided to take the next step straight away.

That night, when it was quite dark, I went up to her mews with a candle. In the flickering light I could see her perched motionless on the screen-perch, standing on one leg, the other hidden in her breast feathers.

Putting the candle down I moved quietly to a position just behind her. Because of the darkness she remained relaxed, only turning her head so that she could watch me with one eye. I took from my pocket a swivel—of the type used on dog leads—and carefully attached both the jesses to it as they hung down behind the perch. I then threaded through the other end of the swivel the leather bootlace which was to be her leash and tied it around the perch at her side. She watched my hands with mild interest but did not move. When she awoke in the morning, she would find herself, at last, fully captive.

I was not there at sunrise, so I do not know whether she simply accepted being tied to her perch or whether she panicked and fought. To assist her in the event of her panicking, I had attached to the underneath of the perch a heavy sack. This was weighted so that it hung down almost to the floor. Thus, if she 'bated'—that is, threw herself off the perch in her panic—first, her jesses would support her and secondly the sacking would be there for her to climb back up to her perch. At any rate, by the time I arrived with her morning feed she appeared to have accepted the situation philosophically, and even bounced a few times in anticipation of her food.

I left her on her perch all day, and heard no sounds of beating wings, which would have meant 'bating'. Towards the end of the afternoon I took the first step in the next big operation: that of introducing her to my fist as a desirable place to perch. In preparation for this I had been wearing an ordinary string glove on my left hand while feeding her, so she was already used to it and even associated it, perhaps, with food.

12

The idea was to get her onto my fist in such a way that it was her idea. I could have picked her up bodily and stuck her there, holding her jesses to prevent escape, but this would certainly have frightened her. And it proved to be so simple. Her way with pieces of meat too big to gobble was to hold them firmly in one foot—'hand' I should say—while tearing pieces off with her beak. So this time, instead of letting her take a sizeable piece of meat from the gloved fingers of my hand, I held on to it, firmly. For a few seconds she tugged at it with her beak, then seemed to realize that it wasn't coming. After glaring at it for a moment she returned to the assault and, to my joy, placed one foot against my forefinger to gain a better purchase.

I let her eat two pieces like that. When I offered the third, there was a difference: my hand was a fraction further from the perch, and about two inches above it. Remember the item of hawk-psychology? It worked. Finding it a little too high to treat in the same manner, she stepped up onto my fist and really got down to the job.

The next few days were taken up with advancing this exercise. This I did, gradually again, by beginning to move her around her mews as she perched on my fist. At first back at her perch by the time she finished her piece of meat, so that she could step back on to it, but soon that became unnecessary and she began to spend the whole meal period on my fist.

We progressed from walking around the room to going downstairs and around the house. At every innovation, every new room, she would stop feeding, feathers flattened in apprehension; but after staring round with button-eyes she would relax visibly and continue her meal.

I began to drag out her meals: made her wait between morsels, gave her some sinewy pieces to sort out, and so on. At the same time I introduced her to the great outdoors.

Her initial reaction to nature was—to put it mildly—traumatic. While she was dealing with an obstinate piece of almost pure ligament, I moved gently out of the back door. For perhaps thirty seconds she continued to assault her food savagely; then she looked up.

I found it almost impossible not to laugh. I had seen her with feathers flattened before, but never like this. She seemed to shrink to half her size and dropped the piece of meat decisively. Even her head shrank, while her eyes seemed to grow until they positively bulged. Her grip on my fist clenched and she leaned back slightly. In that state of cataplexy we spent an unhappy two minutes in the warm summer air before returning indoors—to safety. After peering around anxiously and up at the reassuring ceiling, she roused her feathers in relaxation and looked at my pocket for the next piece of meat.

It did not last very long, however, and within days she was going for long walks during her protracted meals, and was beginning to unbutton a little: every now and again she would 'rouse'—always a sign of contentment in a hawk—the feathers lifting until she looked like someone's fluffy toy.

It is hard to divide her training into headings and sub-headings, it was such a gradual progress. But whenever I felt discouraged I had only to think back to a few weeks before, to a spitting, hissing bundle of hostility crammed into a corner with beak agape and one foot held up and I felt much better.

It was high time that Neeka met her weathering block; the weather was fine most days and I wanted her out in the air. Hawks thrive on life in the open, provided they are protected from strong sunlight, wind and heavy rain or winter weather. In the open the true falcons live on 'blocks', like the one illustrated. Hawks—that is 'shortwings'— need a 'bow perch' since they tend to perch on branches, while falcons always prefer rocks and posts to horizontal branches.

Perhaps this is the time to clear up the matter of the use of the word 'hawk'. It is ambivalent in that while it is used to refer to all the raptors normally trained to the fist, it is also used to describe the 'shortwings'—Sparrow-hawk and Goshawk—as distinct from the 'longwings'—the true falcons. Thus the falconer, with his Peregrine or his Merlin, can refer casually to his 'falcon' or his 'hawk': while the austringer with his shortwing can refer to it only as his 'hawk'. While the kestrel is often looked down upon

Fast asleep with a very full crop...

as 'the beginner's hawk', she is nevertheless a true falcon, a longwing, cousin to the Peregrine and the Gyr, the bird of kings. This denigration of the little kestrel is nothing new: the code of falconry, as laid down in the fifteenth century Boke of St. Albans, assigned each bird of prey to its proper social station. The eagle was to the Emperor, the Gyrfalcon to the King; the prince and the ensuing nobles were allotted the peregrine falcon, but under different names so as to preserve the impression of social distinction. Even the lowly priest was allowed a sparrowhawk, but the poor kestrel was confined to 'knaves'. By association, it would seem, the word kestrel—under various disguises—was used as an adjective referring to all kinds of unpleasant characteristic: 'the cowardly and coistrell rabble' and so on. This meaning of the word, fortunately, fell into disuse, and the kestrel has risen socially. Although too small to fly at any quarry larger than the sparrow and occasionally the starling, she will do almost anything that a peregrine will—even the breath-taking 'stoop' with closed wings. A friend of mine saw a display at one of the Game Fairs; it was given by a young man with two kestrels. He flew each one 'to the lure' (described later) in front of hundreds of people. Although a seasoned falconer, my friend was spell-bound at the flight of these little kestrels as they waited on, then stooped, threw up and stooped again. There, obviously, was training at its best.

Back to Neeka and her weathering-block. In the usual way, I had left the block in her mews for a few days so that she would become used to it. Then, one morning, I set the block up in the garden and took her out to it. I attached her leash to the ring at the base, tying my first falconer's knot in anger. (I had been practising the night before).

When she found herself actually standing on the block she spent some minutes staring down at the wood beneath her feet before daring to move. But soon she shuffled her feet, roused and began looking around her. Nothing missed her attention, from a ladybird climbing a grass-blade three feet away to an aeroplane passing a mile overhead.

I went indoors to get on with some work, but did so whence I could watch her from a window. I was glad that I did, for otherwise I would have missed a delightful scene. After leaning forward and staring intently at the ground beneath her, she suddenly jumped from her block onto the grass. She had a circle with a radius of the length of her leash to explore, and this she did with growing enthusiasm. Starting with cautious steps and frequent pauses, she went on to large hops with brief pauses, and finished up in a *moto perpetua* of wild abandon: dashing backwards and forwards, attacking stalks of grass, digging up soil, dust-bathing energetically—everything in fact except lying on her back and kicking her legs in the air like the amorous Kagu of New Caledonia, that least inhibited of all birds. At length, evidently exhausted by her efforts, she regained her block with a flurry of wings and roused cheerfully.

There is a lurking sensation of guilt at taking a wild creature from freedom into captivity which is much assuaged by moments like these. When she roused and sat relaxed, radiating interest and goodwill, I felt that I had been able to give her something in return for her freedom—that she was truly coming to terms with her new way of life. And as often as that guilt-feeling returns, some little action or look of hers dispels it again.

On looking back at this incident, it occurs to me that it was almost the first view of Neeka the clown. Another example was to follow the next day.

I had read in the manual of the importance of allowing falcons to bathe. When she had been 'ramaging' in my parents' shed I had put a bath in for her, although I never saw any signs of its use. Since then, however, she had not seen a bath, and this was clearly the time to remedy the situation. I chose a big earthenware salad-bowl—from her native village, as it happens—and half-filled it with water. Not knowing quite what to expect, I carried it out into the garden and set it down in front of her block, then retired to watch.

To my amazement, she hesitated only a few seconds before literally leaping into it. The splash caused by her landing was nothing compared with what followed: she literally thrashed about in it, wallowing luxuriously and sending up fountains of spray with flailing wings. After a few minutes of this she stood up, jumped out of the dish, ran a few steps across the grass, turned round, ran back and jumped in again. More spray, then another running jump, and another. At last, when there was hardly any water left in the bowl, she regained her block—with some difficulty—and settled down to dry. It was almost impossible to recognize her: soaking wet as she was her feathers were either plastered down tight or sticking out in irregular tufts. It was quite impossible not to laugh: I had never realized quite how skinny she was beneath her plumage, and her head looked too big for her body. Half-an-hour later, when I looked, she had her back to the sun, her wings hung out to dry, one each side of the block.

One result of this first official bath was to bring her feathers out into a new glory of colours. In the evening sunlight the feathers of her back and wing-coverts were a rich golden-sienna with black crescents appearing towards her tail and flight-feathers. The soft breast feathers were a creamy ochre with streaks of burnt umber growing down from the throat and ending in blurred half-moons around the 'trousers' that covered her thighs. Her flight-feathers gleamed vandyke brown with delicate chestnut edges, while her tail feathers were a beautiful dove-grey with black at their tips.

At this exact point—at the end of her tail—I come to the one sad omission: the thin, almost-white line that should have edged the black band was missing, frayed away during her short stay in the cage while in Alora. Since then some over-enthusiastic preening had further reduced her tail, and all I could do was await her second moult, when these care-worn appendages would be replaced by shiny new ones. Even when she finally has her new tail, in all its glory, I quite expect that she will do something foolish like walking backwards into an electric fire or sitting on a post and getting it chewed by bullocks—I have become used to her with a tatty tail and do not think that I could ever become fully reconciled to a smart one.

After the bath...

Meanwhile, a falcon's job in life should surely be to fly, and progress towards that end was continuing.

Such was her confidence now that she showed great excitement at feeding time, jumping up and down on the spot—'bouncing'—and flapping exuberantly, while watching my hands for the next piece of meat to appear. To start her flying I had only to channel this out-pouring of energy, and this is how I started:—instead of taking her up on to my fist to feed her, I untied her leash and held the end of it in one hand. Then I put a piece of meat on to my glove fist and held it perhaps five inches away from the perch and a little above it. Almost immediately she jumped to my fist. That—in case you hadn't realized—was the first step in training her to fly to my fist.

From then on I offered the meat on my fist progressively further and further from her perch. Soon she had to flap to assist her jump. At last she was actually flying the length of her leash to my fist.

Now I repeated the process from a post, out of doors. At first she was nervous of launching off, but by starting over again with my fist only inches away she soon gathered confidence and would again fly a leash-length for her reward.

At this stage, and without a pause in the daily rhythm of practice, the creance came into use. This is simply a long, light line which replaces the leash on the swivel, allowing the falconer to stand further and further away from his charge; thus she can be encouraged to fly increasing distances for her food without the risk of her being frightened into flying away and perhaps being lost.

At the same time as this work on the creance, Neeka was being carried every day, walked around the countryside being introduced to such things as cars and bicycles and horses and letter-boxes and old ladies with skirts that flap in the wind. The manning was going on and going on well. After the first brief tight-feathered trauma at a speeding lorry or a barking dog she would relax, if watchfully, and rarely bated.

Now, so soon it seemed, she was flying the length of the creance to my fist; about twenty yards, which was all the fishing-line I could find. The great day dawned. No creance. Free as the wind, if she chose.

Like nearly all of these 'great steps forward' it passed off like a normal day. I left her, nervously, sitting on her usual post—it was I who was nervous, by the way, not Neeka—and hurried away to a distance of perhaps ten feet, although it yawned like an abyss between us. Before going on I must try to explain my nerves, explain the enormity of the distance between us. It was because it was the first moment since Paquito caught her in the clump of broom that she had been in the open air without being either tied to her block or attached to my fist by her jesses. Can you understand my feelings now? There was my precious little falcon, of whom I had become so fond, sitting on a post in the middle of a wide landscape, absolutely at liberty to go or stay, just as she wished.

Of course, the second I put a piece of meat on my fist she took off and flew to it like an arrow, landing with her customary squeak of excitement. As she perched on one leg and held her meat daintily in the other, I held my fist up so that I could look at her at eye-level. Her expression was bland, but I was full of happiness: this wild creature full to bursting with the power and beauty of flight had just flown to me, truly free for the first time to take her choice between me and liberty. Emotionally, of course it was a big moment. But any falconer will know that, in fact, I was backing an almost-certain winner: the odds against her flying away must have been hundreds to one against. You could almost say that she knew which side her bread was buttered, which would be quite accurate in an anthropomorphic way.

That was a wonderful period of time, those weeks in September when the weather was kind and Neeka flew further and more strongly every day. Some days were sunny and calm and she would seem to drift down from wherever she perched and float to my fist, landing as light as thistledown. Other days were wild and blustery and she would crouch on my fist, wings half open as she drank the wind, her flight feathers singing. There was no 'drifting' about her flight on days like this: standing a hundred yards upwind, so far that she was hardly visible, I would see her crouch as I raised my fist and then launch into the breeze; she would slice through the moving air—I could see her tail fanning and twisting as the wind buffeted her—and would land exuberantly on my fist with a *thwack* that jolted my arm and then mantle over her meat, defending it from the world.

Between flights she spent her time on the block if the weather was agreeable, and in her mews if not. Sometimes, too, when it was raining or blowing too hard, I would put her on a makeshift perch in my car. She soon came to accept this as the normal thing, which is what I wanted, for the time was approaching when I would have to start moving back to London, and she would be going with me.

As the day approached I made her a 'box-cadge' for travelling on. This was simply a strong cardboard box to which I attached a suitable length of wood as a perch with hessian down each side in case she bated, or fell off.

On our last afternoon before leaving she gave me a fright. As usual I took her down to the disused farm buildings not far from the cottage. Having removed leash and swivel I cast her off from my fist and she flew immediately to her favourite perch, a high wall; upon landing she turned and started craning her neck to watch for the appearance of the first piece of meat. As I walked away, I decided on the spur of the moment to try an experiment: it was an exercise that should properly be performed with the lure, but I decided to try it with the meat on my fist. I showed it to her and she

Trying to pluck up enough
courage to take off...

took off, flying fast and straight towards me. When she was only a few yards away I dropped my arm to my side. Now, the idea was that she should 'throw up'; that is, fly up and circle round over my head, looking for the meat. I saw her brake by throwing her wings and tail forward, in obvious surprise, then begin to gain height, still coming towards me fast. I was just turning my head at the last moment so as to see her bank and begin to circle when she landed on it—the top of my head, that is—with a thud· She got a good grip on my scalp and swore, briefly but distinctly. I persuaded her to return to my fist, and hoping for better results, sent her back to her launching pad.

26

Having a
good scratch~

I went through the same procedure, and this time *was* different. As my hand fell so her face fell—I swear it—and with a mournful expression on her beak she flew slowly past me, without a sideways glance, and went on her way, steadily, towards the distant horizon. Horrified, I started to run after her, but there was no need to panic after all. She appeared to change her mind about the horizon and headed instead for a tall thorn hedge. As if she had forgotten every iota of what she had learnt about flying, she performed an abject belly-flop into the thickest part of it—where it was quite impossible to perch anyway—and lay there awkwardly, spread-eagled on the thorns. When I arrived there beneath her she was peering down at me through the twigs with a hurt expression and flatly refused to move. In the end I had to fetch a wooden box from one of the out-buildings, stand on it and lift her down.

Although I tried with patience, although I called her sweetly, although I stood only six feet away, she refused to raise a feather after that. When I finally gave in she hardly deigned to take the meat from my fingers. We returned home in a dour silence as the daylight, like her confidence in me, faded.

The next morning, when I went in with her breakfast, she bounced so enthusiastically that she actually fell off her perch and had to climb back, beak over fist, before continuing to bounce. I was forgiven.

After the meal I put her on to her cadge and together we left for London.

Chapter Three

LONDON

NEEKA'S introduction to London was a quiet one: she was in a coma at the time. We had left the cottage in a mood of high optimism, but the dual effort of balancing herself and scrutinizing every passing vehicle had its effect on her; when I switched on my side-lights, half-way down the M1, she was dozing and by the time we reached London she was in a deep sleep, her head tucked underneath her wing. On arrival at my flat I carried the cadge in and set it down by the kitchen window; she hardly woke up at all, merely cast a bleary eye around her new surroundings, roused sleepily, and returned her head to its niche beneath her wing.

It was a very different story the following morning. When I had given her half a feed, to take the edge off her appetite, I took her out for a walk along the street. It is a quiet road off Holland Park Avenue, with very little traffic, but Neeka was shattered. The moment I opened the front door and gave her her first daylight view of London she shrank into something resembling a feathered pencil, with a pair of bulging eyes staring in absolute disbelief at everything. The whole thing was too much for her. Thinking that she would relax I began to walk down the street, talking to her in a re-assuring voice. It might have been all right but for a small girl pushing a doll's pram with squeaking wheels. As this monstrous apparition approached, her eyes came even further out of her head; one terrified stare and she bated off my fist as she had never bated before, flying almost horizontally in a frenzy of fear. I put my free hand under her breast and lifted her back to my fist, but she fell off again and then again, as though paralyzed. I headed back home as quickly as I could, and it was all of an hour before she finally relaxed.

That evening, I walked her around indoors and also gave her a few turns around the tiny yard at the back. She seemed a little oppressed by the towering buildings and the walls on all sides, but the session passed off without incident. The following day I made an extension to the outside window-sill overlooking the back yard, and on this I set up a town-version of a weathering-block. Neeka accepted this innovation happily and was soon

David Rode—

fluffed up and relaxed. She spent the whole day outside the window watching aeroplanes passing overhead and threatening the cockney sparrows, who, incidentally, treated her with a familiarity that was humiliating, although I did notice that none of them landed on the windowsill within her reach. They simply carried on with the day's work, from time to time sending loud and derisive chirps in her direction. Splendid birds, these London Sparrers.

That same evening I resorted to a ploy used, I am told, by German falconers many years ago. I took her out after dark and walked around the streets in the lamplight. The reason behind this is simple: that hawks are at their most highly-strung in broad daylight and at their most relaxed in the dark. Under the suffused light of the lamps and in her sleepy condition Neeka sat quietly on my fist as I walked through the empty back-streets. As we passed under each lamp I could see her bright eye cocked towards the buildings as we passed them. I used my body to shield her from possible frights: a man with a dog, a passing motor-cycle and so on. By the time we had arrived back home she was blinking sleepily; within minutes of being returned to her perch she was an unconscious headless bundle of feathers.

It worked, anyway. A couple of trips like that and she appeared to accept the idea of being enclosed all the time, by buildings, by vehicles, by walls, even by people. The fear had gone.

She discovered Holland Park with audible clucks of joy; the green of the grass must have been so refreshing for her. She threatened the small birds that rashly flew across our path and glanced condescendingly at the peacocks. The pigeons made her nervous at first: they are so big and confident and must be at least five times her weight. At this time of year, too, they appear to be all muscle—I can understand her apprehension, they almost frighten me.

She began to show off, and has never stopped since. A small crowd would gather round her and she would go through a repertoire which improved and lengthened with practice: the fierce-hawk-act, all hooked beak and glaring eyes; the supercilious act, glancing at the weather and scratching behind her ear; the relaxed act, rousing her feathers and doing a little preening; a touch of comedy, tripping over her own jesses and almost falling off my fist, and so on, to everyone's delight.

I started to fly her in Holland Park, but found that she would not concentrate if there were people about. Time and again I set her on top of a wall and retired, calling her to me, only to see her turn her back on me and gaze with huge interest at something that was happening on the other side of the wall. The last straw came one day when she humiliated me in public. She had flown twice to my fist, fast and straight, when no-one was looking, so when a small crowd gathered and begged to see her fly, I agreed. I sat

her up on her wall and retired, with our audience, to a distance of thirty yeards or so. Neeka watched us all with interest. I explained to the people what would happen when I raised my fist and whistled and then I raised my fist and whistled. With no hesitation Neeka turned round, lay down and started to have a dust-bath. The crowd dispersed, murmuring politely, and I had to lift her bodily off the top of the wall and stand her up on my fist, where she perched, within a film of dust, in utter contentment.

Wherever I went, within reason, Neeka went too. Sometimes she literally lived in the car: I would go away for a couple of days and take her with me. Where there was no room for her to be properly housed she would stay on her cadge, inside the car by night and on top of its roof by day. She became adept at balancing as I drove, and seemed to glory in speed. Mine was not a fast car, by any means, but when, on a motorway for instance, we went a little faster than usual, she would thrust her head forward and flap her wings excitedly, as though trying to help. Even when fast asleep she would not fall from her perch; she developed a technique of perching along instead of across the perch, with her tail pressed down to act as a third support. When she was asleep like this even sharp braking would hardly shift her—she would merely roll slightly, and perhaps one eye would open for a second or two and then close again.

On long night journeys she would sometimes wake up after three or four hours sleep and 'keep me company'. It was strangely cheering when I turned my head slightly and saw her bright eyes looking back at me. In the dim light of other people's headlights the sharpness of her features was softened so that she looked more like some kind of furry mammal than a hawk.

On one or two of our journeys there was less of this 'togetherness' aspect. One in particular was eventful, and could have ended in a catastrophe. It was only a short journey, down to Surrey to visit my parents. On brief trips I often used to let her free in the car, arranging a sack so that she could perch on the back of the passenger seat, the best vantage point. On this particular trip we had only got as far as Marble Arch when she decided to try my left shoulder as a new perch. I pushed her off absent-mindedly and was severely bitten on the finger. She remounted my shoulder as we swung round into Park Lane; I pushed her off again, with some asperity. On a flood of invective she swept back on board. I clenched my fist, to protect my fingers of course, and pushed her off yet again. Wings flailing and screaming abuse she leapt back and attacked my ear, and so the battle raged. By this time those who had the misfortune to be driving anywhere near my erratically swerving vehicle would have seen within a confused melee of arms and wings, and perhaps would have heard a shrill chattering above the sound of engines.

I won in the end, of course. She retired to her normal perch, muttering and glaring. As if to show her opinion of the whole affair she turned her back on the windscreen and stared moodily out of the rear window. When I accelerated sharply and then touched the brakes so that she had to perform an undignified handstand to keep her balance it was a hollow victory. Relations remained strained until her evening appetite restored her good humour.

After her initial terrified reaction, Neeka settled down quickly. Life at the cottage had been so quiet: she had spent the days on her weathering block and the nights in her own room; she had flown each day, but in the peace of the countryside. Now, in London everything was different: there was noise and bustle, comings and goings at all hours, and even the nights were lit by the street-lamps. In the country I had left her on her block when going out in the car, but in town I was taking her everywhere with me. To get to the park we had to walk through shopping crowds and cross Holland Park Avenue, often packed solid with rush-hour traffic. The peace of even the quietest streets was liable to be torn apart at any moment by a sports car or a crowd of revellers.

Sometimes I would return, having left her in the car, to find it surrounded by curious passers-by; Neeka would be either showing off or ignoring them, but never worried in any way. In short, she was rapidly becoming a Londoner.

Towards the middle of October, after three weeks in London, we went back to the cottage for a spell. The weather was mild, fortunately, although the land was very wet; water lay in the furrows and in broad sheets on some pastures. It was so good to smell the countryside again; Neeka, on her first outing, produced the same soft clucks of pleasure as on her first visit to Holland Park. To my surprise, though, she would not fly at first. I had expected her to revel, immediately, in the free air, but she sat gazing around her cheerfully and made no attempt to move. After a while she flew a short distance to my fist, and then again, but no more. She was cheerful and bright, but simply not interested in flying.

Although I worried for a while, I finally decided that it was because everything was new again—after all, she had been cooped up in London for nearly a month—and that she would get over it quickly.

I was partly right, but not altogether. She did improve, considerably, but not as quickly nor as much as I had anticipated. Although we progressed, I had a nagging feeling that she had been—somehow—retarded, but how or by what I could not fathom.

I introduced her to the lure. This is made of leather stuffed with material around a hard core. It has thin leather thongs on each side and can be attached to a line. Following the rule of gradual introduction I had left it near her perch for several days, before leaving London. On arriving at the cottage, I began to feed her from it, attaching small pieces of meat by the thongs provided. She caught on eagerly, and was soon standing on it pulling the meat off expertly. At the next feed she learned how to jump to it and even fly a couple of feet from her perch to land on it. When I took her out, I flew her to the lure held in my hand, and thus she came to associate it with food. At the end of a week she was showing excitement at the mere sight of it, and I was ready to take the next step.

The following day I attached a line to the lure and took it out to the garden where Neeka was impatiently awaiting her first meal. This time, instead of calling her to it, I untied her leash and left her on her block. Having attached the meat as usual, I began to drag the lure along the ground towards her. She watched it approach with great excitement, her feathers flattened, her head thrust forward, her shoulders hunched in the attitude of a falcon about to take off. I expected her to leap down on to it as it passed beneath her, but I was wrong. With her eyes bulging almost out of her head she watched it pass without doing anything to stop it. Her resistance snapped, however,

as it began to bump over the grass away from her: she half-flew, half-leaped the four feet or so and landed on it with a high-pitched squeak of excitement. The next time she leaped as it passed beneath her. By the end of the session she was going to it almost as soon as I placed it on the ground. During the days that followed she learned to fly down to it from different perches and at varying distances, and at last was ready to come properly 'to the lure'.

This exercise has three main functions. One: to train a hawk in the art of chasing an elusive quarry. Two: to get it fit. And three: to call it back to the falconer after a flight. Up to this time I had trained Neeka to fly to my fist, but then she had never flown from a distance greater than, say, a hundred yards. The use of the lure is designed to bring back a falcon that may be flying a thousand feet above. It is swung around in a circle, on the end of a light line, and invariably has meat attached to it, as a reward. When it is used to call a falcon back, the bird is allowed to 'catch' it immediately; while she eats the meat, the falconer makes in to her quietly and takes her up on his fist. When it is used to exercise the hawk, however, the falconer continues to swing it; as the hawk pursues it he can vary the speed and pitch so as to make it more difficult. An experienced falconer can keep the lure free of the pursuing hawk for quite some time. An experienced falcon, on the other hand, becomes amazingly adept, and the falconer is lucky to keep the lure clear of her for even a short while.

I did not get to this stage with Neeka. In the time left before I had to return to London, she learned to fly simply to the swung lure, but I had to release it and allow her to

land on it—nothing I did could persuade her to fly after it in circles. If I continued to swing it she would simply fly away again and perch somewhere, as if she could not be bothered.

I was disappointed, of course. Remember that I was doing all this out of a book, with no previous experience to guide me. It occurred to me then that neither was she flying as well as her early efforts had promised. For a while I had no idea where I was going wrong, but then a glimmer of light showed in the darkness and a theory began to form. At that time it was only the beginning of an idea, but it has grown steadily and I am now fairly satisfied that it is correct.

The development of this theory was aided by yet another failure, albeit a hilarious one. You must have seen pictures of falcons 'hooded', often in beautifully worked hoods with plumes at their crown. Although so decorative, they are strictly functional: they keep their wearers 'in the dark', literally, and so prevent them being frightened or trying to fly too soon, or at the wrong quarry. Although Neeka did not need a hood— she was too well manned, and too small to take quarry—I decided to train her to the hood anyway, as an experience for both of us.

A falconer friend had made me a kestrel-sized hood: a mistake, since Neeka was approximately half the size of an English kestrel. The early stages passed off normally, with Neeka taking scraps of meat initially from the outside and finally from the inside of the hood itself. I decided to take the big step one mild afternoon in November. Neeka was sleepy and everything seemed propitious. We were out in the garden at the time. I let her take a couple of pieces of meat from inside the hood and then, as she was swallowing the third piece, I popped the hood over her head and prepared myself for trouble.

She sat as though frozen. As gently as I could, I pulled the thong at the back of the hood which tightened it, and then waited for her reaction. After perhaps a minute she moved her head two degrees to the left, experimentally; then four degrees to the right. Another minute's immobility and then she tried looking down slightly. She was not frightened; her feathers were neither down nor up. But she was obviously puzzled as to why the lights had suddenly gone out. After another two or three minutes' immobility she appeared to come to a decision. In one swift movement she raised her right foot, hooked a toe beneath the back of the hood and flipped it neatly off her head on to the ground. She stared down at it briefly and then proceeded to forget the whole incident. glancing meaningfully at my pocket for the next piece of meat.

There was nothing about this in the text book, so I had to work out my own solution. I replaced the hood and waited for her to try to remove it. After a much shorter period she again raised her right foot, and as she did so I moved my fist sharply to one side: the result was, of course, that she lost her balance and the foot came down again in a wild grab. From then on, every time she tried to lift her foot to remove the hood, I repeated the movement, and in the end she gave up and sat still.

Now, I thought, *that's got you*. I began to walk, watching her carefully, and stopped when I saw her head begin to move. It was moving in a most peculiar way, oscillating

Neeka's ridiculous 'Preening face'...

very slowly as though on a ball and socket joint. As I watched the movement became more exaggerated, with a sort of lurch towards one side. I was more puzzled than alarmed until this strange performance came to a climax and she toppled forwards off my fist to hang inert from her jesses. Suddenly, terrified lest she should have been choked to death I lifted her on to my left hand and slipped the hood off: in a flash she was on her feet and attacking the offending item, holding it firmly in one foot and tearing at the little feathers with her beak, chattering with rage.

I tried again when she was sitting on a brick wall, thinking that this might prove easier to balance on. This time there was no oscillation of her head, she simply began to bow forwards and down, very slowly, until her head came to rest on the surface, in front of her feet. And there she stayed, absolutely still. As I looked at her, in this ridiculous pose, the laughter burst out of me—she reminded me irresistibly of the great Schultz's Charlie Brown, leaning his head against a wall in utter dejection. I lifted her and removed it once again, this time right away from her so that she could not attack it. I have never tried again. I think perhaps the hood was too heavy for her—it was certainly too big or it would not have slipped off so easily, even with the thongs tight. But it was rather a pity in a way; while she was sitting erect and motionless with it on, she did look rather splendid.

If the hood episode was a failure, another experiment was a marked success. Ever since wanting to keep a falcon I had nurtured the idea of carrying one on horseback, as in the days of chivalry. I already had the horse, at livery in the nearby village of Old Dalby, and here I was with a manned falcon. I decided not to delay any longer.

Originally I had intended taking her hooded to accustom her to the movement, but this clearly was impracticable. I hoped that she would accept the idea nevertheless; and especially since noticing how quickly she had grown used to things in the bustle and noise of London.

She had already met horses and by now appeared quite blasé in their presence. When I mounted mine and a friend passed her up to me she was only tight-feathered for a matter of seconds before relaxing. We set off at a sedate walk and Neeka had no trouble in maintaining her balance—indeed, there was very little movement of my fist to disturb her—but when we went forward into a trot she found it less easy. My 'posting' to the trot gave my fist a rising and falling motion, and for some little while she was uneasy, flapping her wings intermittently to aid her balance, and looking around her nervously. But in a little while she settled to it and began to ride the movement. Now, too, she began to enjoy the wind in her face and the changing scenery. The mare was superb, bless her; which was fortunate, because I was reduced to riding her with one hand.

We walked again and Neeka roused once and then mantled, stretching one beautiful wing at a time and fanning her tail feathers. She appeared so relaxed that when we came to an open grass field I decided to risk everything on a canter. I gave her a short distance at the trot to readjust to movement, and then squeezed the mare on into a steady canter.

The result was electrifying; I felt the needle-prick of Neeka's claws as her grip tightened on the glove and then she was almost flying into the wind. As the big mare surged forward over the ridge-and-furrow the little falcon crouched low on my fist, head thrust forward and wings open and tense, yet still. Her beak was slightly open and her eyes looked fiercer than I had ever seen them. It was a thrilling experience and a wonderful conjunction of two things that I love; the fierce beauty of a falcon on my fist and the powerful surge of a thoroughbred horse between my legs and on the bit. Say what you like, I believe that some ancient things are good—and perhaps even valid in a world in which they appear anachronistic.

Two days after the ride we were back in London. I mentioned, a little way back, a theory that had begun to form in my mind concerning Neeka's disappointing lack of progress in the art and craft of flying. Briefly, it was this: Neeka was becoming too tame. It occurred to me, at the time, that a hunting falcon must stay half-wild in order to keep its aggressive instincts; that the sight of food, actual or prospective, must elicit an immediate and unvarying response; to catch it, killing if necessary. Neeka—or so I believed—had become too relaxed, too confidential, too *human*. The inference was clear; that as far as training a falcon, *for falconry*, is concerned, I had not done very well. But I felt a little better as I came to realise something else: perhaps Neeka was no trained falcon, but what a character she was becoming and how delightfully relaxed in almost any situation!

Back in London she appeared to be enjoying every moment of city life. Come to think of it, she was born amidst the bustle and noise of a flourishing Spanish village, so why shouldn't she?

She began to form relationships with local tradespeople and especially with Dave Steel, the butcher. I used to take her with me when buying her food; inside the shop she became almost apoplectic with greed. Once she caught me unawares, leaned over and caught hold of a side of beef, intending to take it away with her. She swore bitterly when I made her let go but Dave slipped her a piece of kidney and all was forgotten.

I continued to introduce her to new situations, taking her on to buses and trains, into shops and even local pubs. I took her into my publishers' one day and right into the office of one of the directors. She behaved well until I stood up to leave and then disgraced herself by 'slicing a mute' (as the jargon so delicately has it) right across the top of his desk, papers and all.

43

A ferocious attack on an
unsuspecting chunk of beef —

PEL

In the country she had often sat out in the rain quite happily, but all that had changed. Sitting indoors I would hear a sudden flurry and a banging on the window: going into the other room to investigate I would find that it was Neeka knocking to be let in on account of a light shower. On the occasions when I refused to let her in she would stand outside with her face pressed against the glass, glaring at me in speechless fury. After a while she would go back to her block, but instead of facing outwards, as usual, she would sit facing the interior and keep up a steady reproachful stare until the rain stopped.

At about this time she did something else that I have never been able to explain. There was a cold spell with the temperature at night falling well below zero. As she was from a warmer climate I brought her into my living room to sleep, putting her perch on top of a cupboard. In spite of the light being on, she would go to sleep in the usual way: one foot hidden in her breast-feathers and her head over her shoulder. Then, one night, I happened to glance up at her and noticed something odd: as I watched I saw that she was gradually leaning further and further back. I waited for her to correct it, or wake up, but no: she reached an angle of about seventy degrees and then fell backwards off the perch. She woke with a jerk and a startled squawk and climbed rapidly back to her perch where she sat muttering to herself and casting angry looks in my direction, as though I had somehow been the cause of the accident. After that I saw her do it three or four times, always in her sleep; I have never understood the cause.

One day I was watching her out on her block—or rather off her block, for she was stalking a minute insect across the window-ledge—when it occurred to me how often she made me laugh. On analysing this thought, I realized that it was surprising, because my preconception of a relationship with a falcon had not included laughter. Yet thinking back, almost to the beginning, I remembered being made to laugh: at Neeka hopping from foot to foot as a procession of ants passed over them; at Neeka scuttling like an overgrown mouse across the floor of the shed, and so on. So it had been there right from the beginning, this comical aspect; moreover it appeared to be developing fast, yet it could change so quickly to something else. Just as I am in the middle of a fit of laughter at some action of hers she will suddenly change: her feathers flatten and she crouches and all at once she is no longer a clown, but beautiful and dangerous. This is a kind of paradox which persists, even now—only now I am used to it and accept it.

There are so many aspects of my relationship with her—comfort from her company; pride in her training; amusement at her comicality; a kind of awe when she flies, for she is so beautiful then; even a kind of fear when she crouches over a piece of meat, for she is fiercer than I. And my reactions towards her change as she switches from one aspect to another, and that can happen very quickly indeed.

A good shake after preening~ Dee

For a long time I felt a sense of guilt after laughing at her, but at last I realized the truth; Neeka is *far* too small to be dignified.

Chapter Four

THE London life continued through November and into December. As Neeka became more and more at home in town, so my visions receded of a trained falcon waiting on overhead. Our life together became a matter of complete understanding, and I would take her around town with as much worry as if she were a brief case or a book in my hand. I became adept at keeping my keys and my money in right-hand pockets (while she occupied the left hand) and at dodging stray 'mutes' that might threaten my shoe. We took our daily walks in Holland Park or Hyde Park, or just around the streets. Life was settling into a steady pattern when something happened to turn everything upside down.

In the middle of December I left the country for a week and Neeka went to some friends who have a large house already half-full of contented animals. When I got back they told me that she had met with an accident. She had been allotted a screen perch in a loose box. One afternoon she managed to undo the knot in her leash and flew up to look out of the window, as she had done in her early days at the cottage. But here there was no windowsill for her to sit on. She probably clung for a while to the narrow ledge and then turned to fly back to her perch, but one jess had caught on a nail and she found herself hung up. In her panic she twisted and flapped for who knows how long before they came with her evening meal. There was no blame, it could have happened in my care just as easily.

When I saw her she appeared quite normal in herself but she was using only her good leg, the right one. The other was raised and pointed outwards, almost at right angles to her body. She was feeding normally and could even sit on my fist, on one leg, but soon tired.

I took her to a vet. He examined the leg thoroughly and assured me that there was no break and no dislocation. He said that she should get the use of it back, but that it might remain somewhat twisted. Some days later she began to use it again, if somewhat gingerly, and I felt a great sense of relief.

My relief was premature. Ten days after the accident her right foot—her good one —began to swell. I ignored it and hoped for the best, but after a week it was twice its

Using her glorious wings to full
advantage in a tug-of-war...

David Reid-

normal size and the swelling began to move up the leg. She began to show symptoms of pain in the swollen foot, moving it restlessly and sometimes pecking at it. She had always slept perching on one leg; now she began to lie down, like a young bird before it leaves the nest. At first she would stand up much of the day-time, but her periods of lying became longer until at last she remained down all the time.

At this point, as the Manual instructed, I took her back to the vet. He explained that this swelling was probably due to her whole weight being taken on the one foot, and was therefore inevitable. He could find no favourable point at which to lance the abscess but gave me some penicillin to give her in her meat and advised that she be kept on something soft so as to relieve the pressure on her foot. On the way back from the surgery, instead of carrying her on my closed fist I placed her on my open hands; she settled down straight away, lying in my cupped palm, her tail sticking out over my fingertips and her beak resting on my wrist. By the time I arrived at my front door she was asleep; even through the glove I could feel her warmth and her heart beating. Looking down at her nestling in my hand I felt more than ever before the responsibility of having taken her from the nest, for now she depended on me utterly.

That was a bad time. Most of the day she would be lying down but sometimes she would try to stand, and it was a pitiful sight. To put her weight on her right foot was painful, yet when she tried to take her weight on the other leg it collapsed, and she would fall sideways. Every time this happened I felt something akin to physical pain, yet there was nothing I could do but wait for the swelling to come to a head, or go down. For some days it did neither, but continued to creep up her leg.

The worst time was at night. I do much of my work by night, and I kept her with me all the time, with a screen to keep the light out of her eyes. At times the pain would seem to become unendurable and she would suddenly attack her own foot, biting at it savagely until I stopped her. In the daytime the pain would seem to ease and I would place her near the window, on a discarded shirt. Here she would lie all day looking out at the sky. Of course, she could no longer eat her food in the normal way, holding it down firmly and tearing at it, and I had to cut her meat into small pieces and give it to her in my fingers.

I could see her running down, like a clock to which the key has been lost. I had to watch her lying more and more still; watch her reactions slowing down; her eyes losing their roundness and their lustre, becoming slightly oval in shape; her appetite fading until she was only picking listlessly at morsels. The only time she moved with any animation was when she attacked her own leg, swollen almost up to the hock now. Afterwards she would just lie, her beak resting on the material in front of her. I knew that I was watching her die.

Yet somehow she did not die. I don't know when the turning point came, but I remember a period when I almost began to hope, without any reason except perhaps that things had stopped getting worse. For two days she seemed to hover on the edge of something. During that time I kept as quiet as I could and moved softly, for I had the feeling that any little thing would push her over the edge, so faint was her heartbeat— so thin the thread.

The beginning of the road was clearly marked for she stood up. It was a brief and unsteady effort, but she stood up and then shook herself, like a dog coming out of the water. The effort made her lose her balance and sit down with a bump, but it was at that moment that I relaxed and stopped being afraid.

Lest my feelings seem out of proportion to the situation, let me explain: there was a little more to it than merely an animal's sickness; there was that responsibility, hanging over me like the sword of Damocles, that *I* had taken her from the nest.

It was all past, anyway. The swelling began to recede—in fact the whole procedure reversed itself. She still spent much of her time lying down, keeping her weight off the still painful foot, but the trend was in the right direction. It was around this point that a quality began to show itself in Neeka's character that I had never fully appreciated; she was a fighter. Although still a cripple she was not begging for crutches. She started to get around, unbelievably. Even in perfect health falcons move, when on the ground, with a comical half-hopping, half-running gait. Neeka now began to move in a parody of this gait. With wings flapping and an eager expression she would shuffle unevenly across the floor to where she was going. Once there she would sit down for a minute, looking cheerful, and then shuffle back to where she had come from. Sometimes she would topple forward precipitately, and I would hear a sharp 'tap' as her beak hit the wooden floor, followed by a short expletive; she would then get up and continue unsteadily on her way. It was while watching one of these performances that the nickname 'Shufflebottom the Unsteady' came to my mind. Although far steadier nowadays, it has died hard, and there is something about plain 'Shufflebottom' that suits her perfectly.

It showed at feeding time too; she would swallow the first few pieces from my fingers, but then she would try to get hold of a piece in her right foot to tackle it in the normal way. It was fascinating to watch her solve this problem—and remember that her left leg was now twisted out so that she could not use it for holding meat, and neither would it support her weight. So she had only one foot for holding her food, and then no leg left to stand on. She solved it, after much experimenting, by supporting herself on her wings. She used them just like legs, with her tail fanned out as a steadier, while holding the meat in her right foot and pulling at it as before.

I began to realize that she was going to have to overcome a number of similar problems. Like a man who has lost a limb, she would have to learn new ways of doing almost everything; for even if the right foot healed completely, the left leg would always remain twisted and unreliable.

Meanwhile, now that I could relax and enjoy her again, I was beginning to notice things that had escaped me during the bad period. For example, I mentioned that she had reverted to the juvenile method of sleeping, lying down instead of perching. She was still lying down much of the time, and I began to notice how many different positions she was adopting. I would never have believed it possible for a mere bird to find so many variations on the simple theme of lying down. I began to draw her in her sleep and soon had so many different sketches that they took on the appearance of a collection.

Anticipating a further improvement, I had put her block down beside the old shirt on which she rested; sure enough I came in one day to find her perched up on it. Certainly she was half-sitting, with her tail helping to support her, but she was up on her block looking happy and it was another stride forward.

Somewhere along the line she had lost the idea of going to sleep in the evening and waking up in the morning. In the old days she had gone to sleep at nightfall even if we were travelling, but at some point during her illness she had obviously become confused. I noticed that she was beginning to wake up towards midnight, and thereafter

Her regular sparring-partner—

have spells of dozing interspersed with periods of wakefulness. At daybreak she would liven up considerably, but at about 10.00 a.m. she would fall into a deep sleep. So like a child kept up past its usual bedtime.

She began to show signs of excess energy, playing like a kitten with anything she could lay her beak on. She would attack a piece of paper and tear it to pieces, or simply rush about as though looking for something. I put her outside on the window-ledge for the first time in a fortnight and was rewarded by seeing her take an immediate and vigorous dust-bath that must have lasted for nearly ten minutes. Everything happening so quickly using her legs more every day, stronger and more lively all the time, yet in spite of all this something was wrong. Only this time it was something wrong with me.

After all the anxiety of the 'bad times' and the relief at her recovery, I seemed to experience a sudden reaction. Looking back, I still find it hard to define this particular malaise: it was something to do with her loss of grace. Not in the usual meaning of the expression—I mean her loss of *gracefulness*. Before her accident, and the ensuing complications, there had been so much about her that was graceful. Apart from her moments of comicality, her movements had all been like a ballet-dancer's, a blend of tension and repose. She had been a joy to watch, even when preening herself or simply looking around her; there had been the falcon's tensility and suppleness and some of its erect dignity. And now what?

Poor little crippled bird, with one twisted leg and one still-tender foot, hobbling and flopping about. Every time her falcon-nature made her attempt some action that

55

had once been smooth and graceful, she fell over. One day she tried to mantle: her wing stretched out and down, her tail fanned; I held my breath as she started to stretch her leg after the wing; the whole beautiful thing was building up to that moment of extreme tension when the outspread wing trembles like a butterfly's in the sun . . . and of course she collapsed in an ungainly heap as her twisted leg betrayed her.

It was a kind of bitterness that I was feeling; a futile anger at all that lost beauty. And if this reaction, also, seems out of proportion, remember that I had spent much of my time drawing her, and was therefore doubly aware of the loss of those visual qualities.

It passed quickly, forced away by admiration for the sheer guts of her approach to it all. So, she fell over trying to preen her tail feathers: so, all right, she would try again and again until she managed it, even if she had to use both her wings to supplement her legs. She was unabashed by the magnitude of any problem; she just went at it, all stops out. How could I mope around the place with this all-action, go-go-go bird on the premises? Inevitably, she pulled me back out of my depression.

One morning in January the day dawned clear and sunny with a snap of frost. Neeka awoke with a little extra bounce and suddenly I wanted to see her fly again. I put some meat in my pocket, took her up and out to the car and we went to Hyde Park. It was about eight o'clock on a weekday morning; a few people were out with their dogs, but a long way off. As I walked across the grass, still dusted with frost, she crouched excitedly on my fist. She had adapted her stance (of course) and was fairly secure; it was good to feel the needle-prick of her talons again, and from both feet too. She looked around, seemingly at all points of the compass at once, feathers half-tight, half-fluffed in a mixture of excitement and pleasure. I found a convenient branch on a lone tree and set her up on it. She sat stiffly upright, her eyes darting everywhere, drinking in the distance and the green grass. Slowly I walked away from her to a range of sixty yards or so. When I turned and looked back I could hardly see her. I held out a piece of meat on my fist and started to call her, but slowly, in no hurry. It had been a long time and I was prepared to wait.

After a long time, in which I was not impatient, she came. Suddenly she was flying fast towards me. As she approached I could see her bullet-like shape and her wings like knife-blades cutting the air. Even closer I saw her tail twist and flick back as she corrected a slight drift, saw the fierce beak and the black eyes and then the wing-surface broaden as she began to brake, the tail feathers brought down, the yellow legs thrust forward and *thwack*! on my fist with a little scream of excitement and she was fluttering over her meat, a falcon again.

Now I know that not all the beauty is lost. There is nothing wrong with her wings.

Chapter Five

NOW it is spring and Neeka is one year old. She has just completed her first moult and looks much smarter than before, although I must wait until her next moult for her new tailfeathers. One rather shattering fact has emerged, indicated by the appearance of the first blue-grey feather on her head: Neeka is a boy.

After the inevitable mental confusion caused by this item, I was soon able to absorb it and adjust to it. Fortunately it is normal in falconry to refer to both sexes in the feminine, so Neeka is still a 'she'. On the other hand it does explain a great deal: her comical antics, her inability to be serious for any length of time and so on. I find it easy now to be aware of Neeka as a 'he' while yet referring to 'her' in conversation.

It does raise all manner of interesting conjecture: she *was* the largest of the three eyasses, so she *should* have been a female. What went wrong? Perhaps she was from another, earlier brood and was merely visiting, who knows? Neeka guards her (his) secret.

She has, as I expected, fully adapted to her 'gammy' leg. When on the ground she moves in squat frog-like hops and sits down frequently and not always intentionally. In the air she is more skilled than before and is flying to me now from distances at which she is quite invisible, appearing as a low moving speck against the background and growing at last to recognizable proportions before landing on my fist with the usual squeak.

On a recent visit to our cottage in Leicestershire I flew her in a blustery wind. She was managing quite well when she was caught by a violent gust and I was treated to the sight of Neeka being blown steadily backwards while flapping frantically in an effort to get back to the safety of my fist. At last she gave up the attempt and dropped to the ground; when I went to recover her, I found her crouching in a deep hoof-print, peering anxiously over the edge to ensure that I was on my way.

In London she continues to fly in Hyde Park except when the weather is bad. If it is raining I often fly her indoors: she perches on the edge of the sink in the kitchen and I go into the next room and call her: seconds later she comes rocketing through the

David Rook

doorway, her eager face looking this way and that to see whereabouts I am standing. After a few early misses she achieved a high degree of skill and now makes only an occasional mistake. Sometimes she becomes rather cocky and cuts her angle too fine coming through the door; when this happens one wing-tip flicks the door-jamb and she performs two or three horizontal cart-wheels before landing indignantly on her bottom. As always, it is *my* fault and she scolds me as she flies up to my fist to try again.

Now that the weather is improving she is spending all day and part of the night outside the window. Diplomatic relations with the sparrows have improved enormously, and at times there seems to be quite a party going on. Neeka's moult was very popular as its peak coincided with sparrow nest-building time; at one point there was a line of sparrows waiting for the next feather to fall and a sharp scuffle when it did. I find it amusing to think of sparrows lining their nests with hawk-feathers.

A small headline in the *Telegraph* caught my eye some time ago: 'KESTREL SEEN TO CAPTURE SPARROW'. I cut it out, re-arranged it a little and mounted it tastefully. It now adorns Neeka's perch and reads: 'SPARROW SEEN TO CAP- TURE KESTREL'. As a result of all this co-existence outside the kitchen-window, my imagination is beginning to play tricks on me. Are the sparrows in Portland Rd. really developing hooked beaks? At any rate, of one thing I am certain: Neeka is quite definitely beginning to chirp.

Her character has developed astonishingly since her first summer and she is a bundle of paradoxes; two examples will illustrate what I mean:—

Sometimes she looks so fluffy and toy-like that I absent-mindedly put out my hand to stroke her and get severely bitten, yet if I leave her untied and go into the next room it is only minutes before there is a tapping on the door between the two rooms; if the door is ajar feathers will appear in the crack and when at last I open it she will fly up to my fist immediately, overjoyed at the reunion.

Once, when she was being particularly unco-operative I tried to discipline her by flipping a finger across her beak—to my astonishment she went for me hammer and tongs, flying at my chest and trying to squeeze the breath out of me with her little hands, each at least an inch long. Yet again, while shaping up to deliver the *coup-de-grace* to a sleepy blue-bottle, it had the bad taste to buzz at the wrong moment, fright-ening poor Neeka out of her wits. In fact she was very badly frightened by one of her own feathers the other day; she had left it lying a foot away from her when the breeze blew it suddenly towards her; she baled out immediately and thus avoided this vicious and unwarranted attack.

Neeka now has a companion: a tawny owl named Edgar. After a traumatic intro-duction, during which Edgar (who is an owl of very little brain) mistook Neeka for his

breakfast, and tried to swallow her, they have settled down very well together. Occasionally Edgar gets absent-minded and tries to do it again: Neeka, who has no intention of being swallowed, points this out vigorously and the *status quo* is restored.

So life in London goes on for Neeka, on the go from dawn to dusk, every day packed with incident. I sometimes wonder, nowadays, how I ever managed without a bird around the house.

By the way, I have a message for those two crows who keep frightening the wits out of my little falcon by chasing her round and round Hyde Park: I'm going to Spain next month, back to Neeka's birthplace. When I return to England, I shall be bringing reinforcements with me. Those crows had better watch out then.

Dust bathing—

Epilogue

NOW, after telling the story of Neeka, I must make a plea:—To anyone who finds the idea of a falcon-about-the-house attractive, *please* do *not* just go out and buy one. It is quite possible to do so: one can buy hawks of many species from dealers and it is a trade which I deplore. There are two reasons for my asking this, and the first deals with conservation.

Birds of prey all over the world are declining rapidly. Many American species face extinction, such as the Everglade kite and the beautiful swallow-tailed kite. In Great Britain we have seen the Golden Eagle and the kite reduced to a few pairs in Scotland and Wales respectively. The once-common sparrow-hawk is now seen only in certain parts of the country. Even the glorious peregrine, once found all round the British coastline, is in deadly danger as more and more eggs fail to hatch, poisoned by toxic agricultural chemicals.

In Britain a licence must be obtained from the Home Office to take any wild hawk; a few licences will be granted for the commoner species and none for the rarer. Most States of the U.S. forbid the capture of the many indigenous species of hawks. This is as it should be. But in some other countries there is no such control. Captured birds are often advertised as 'ideal for falconry' when in fact they are no such thing. Often they live out their lives perching in a cramped cage without ever seeing the sky again. That may sound like an emotional appeal. It is. But it is based on fact.

The second reason why I would ask you not to go out and buy a hawk has to do with responsibility. As I have pointed out, it is easy to obtain one, but then what?

Training a hawk calls for experience with wild animals, care and above all, *time*. It must be properly looked after and exactly fed; they are such fragile creatures for all their lordly looks. A hawk must be flown and carried regularly if it is to stay fit and friendly. Any cutting down of the time spent on its training means a slipping-back to its original state of fear and distrust.

This is my greatest fear: that because of this book, someone somewhere will go out and buy a hawk; someone who has insufficient time to train it and lives far from any open space; that this hawk will slowly decline and finally die.

I hope this book has brought home to those previously unaware the beauty and the character of the falcon. I would wish that people everywhere become increasingly aware of the predicament of the birds of prey in this modern world—sympathetically aware.

These fierce, beautiful and diverse creatures have their backs to the wall—give them a little moral support.